Chocolate

Victoria Blakemore

© 2019 Victoria Blakemore

All rights reserved. This book or parts thereof may not be reproduced in any form, stored in any retrieval system, or transmitted in any form by any means—electronic, mechanical, photocopy, recording, or otherwise—without prior written permission of the publisher, except as provided by United States of America copyright law. For permission requests, write to the publisher, at "Attention: Permissions Coordinator," at the address below.

vblakemore.author@gmail.com

Copyright info/picture credits

Cover, Dima Sobko/Shutterstock; Page 3, Dima Sobko/Shutterstock; Page 5, Shulevskyy Volodymyr/Shutterstock; Page 7, dghchocolatier/Pixabay; Page 9, Zichrini/Pixabay; Page 11, bigacis/AdobeStock; Page 13, cook_inspire/AdobeStock; Page 15, Max4e Photo/Shutterstock; Page 17, Alexander Narraina/Shutterstock; Page 19, HandmadePictures/AdobeStock; Page 21, Brent Hofacker/AdobeStock; Page 23; beats_/AdobeStock; Page 25, domnitsky/AdobeStock; Page 27, koss13/AdobeStock; Page 29, am13photo/AdobeStock; Page 31, Africa Studio/AdobeStock; Page 33, fahrwasser/AdobeStock; Page 35, showcake/AdobeStock; Page 37, Storyblocks; Page 39, romerince/AdobeStock; Page 41, dreambigphotos/AdobeStock; Page 43, arekmalang/AdobeStock; Page 45, kobeza/AdobeStock; Page 47, jenslphotography/AdobeStock; Page 49, raptorcaptor/AdobeStock; Page 51, creativefamily/AdobeStock

Table of Contents

What is Chocolate?	2
Ingredients	4
Cocoa Beans	6
Cocoa Butter	8
History	10
Making Chocolate	14
Milk Chocolate	18
Dark Chocolate	20
White Chocolate	22
Nougat	24
Caramel	26
Nuts	28
Truffles	30
Baking	32
Chocolate Milk	34
Hot Chocolate	36
Ice Cream	38
Fudge	40
Nutrition	42
Health Benefits	44
Chocolate Festivals	46
Recipes	48
Glossary	52

What is Chocolate?

Chocolate is a sweet treat that can be eaten on its own or with other ingredients. It is a very popular ingredient in baking and candy-making.

There are two main kinds: dark chocolate and milk chocolate. They differ in their ingredients, color, and sweetness.

Chocolate can be made in a solid form or in a liquid syrup.

Ingredients

Chocolate is made with cocoa butter, sugar, **cocoa liquor**, and **lecithin**. It can also contain vanilla, milk, and other add-ins.

Different kinds of chocolate are made with different amounts of ingredients. By adding different amounts of ingredients, the sweetness can be changed.

Dark chocolate is made with the least amount of sugar. Milk chocolate has more sugar and less **cocoa liquor.**

Cocoa Beans

Cacao beans come from the Theobroma, or cacao, tree. They are found inside large pods that grow on the tree.

Before they can be made into chocolate, the beans must be dried and roasted. Then, they can be ground into a chocolate paste.

Cacao beans are used to make things like chocolate, cocoa powder, and cocoa butter.

Cocoa Butter

Cocoa butter is also called theobroma oil. It is a vegetable fat made from cocoa beans. It has a mild chocolate flavor.

Cocoa butter is used to make chocolate. It helps to give chocolate a hard shape until it melts. It is also used in **ointments** and beauty products.

Cocoa butter is solid at room temperature. It melts just below body temperature, which makes chocolate melt in your mouth.

History

Chocolate was first made by the Olmec, Aztec, and Mayan people of Central America. They would roast cacao seeds, then remove the nib and grind it into a paste.

The chocolate paste would be mixed with hot water. It made a very **bitter** drink.

Cacao nibs are part of cacao seeds. They have been dried, cleaned, roasted, and removed from their shell.

Spanish explorers brought cacao seeds back to Spain with them. The seeds were traded and sold to other countries in Europe.

A Dutch inventor found a way to make cocoa powder from cacao beans. This made chocolate less expensive and available to more people.

Chocolate as we know it was created in 1847. It was made by mixing cocoa butter with cocoa powder. After that, chocolate candies became very popular.

Making Chocolate

Cocoa beans are harvested from the fruit of the cocoa tree. Once the beans are cleaned, they are left for several days to develop their flavor.

Then, the beans are dried and roasted. After they are roasted, the nibs are removed from the cocoa bean shells.

The cocoa nibs are ground down into **cocoa liquor**. This can be made into cocoa powder and cocoa butter.

Once the cocoa powder and cocoa butter are made, other ingredients can be added. **Milk solids**, sugar, and **lecithin** are added to make different kinds of chocolate.

The mixture is then "conched." It is rolled, kneaded, heated, and put into a machine that stirs and smooths the mixture.

Chocolates can be molded into different shapes. They can also be topped with fruits and nuts.

Milk Chocolate

Milk chocolate was first made by a Swiss man named Daniel Peter in the late 1800's. He made it by adding milk to the usual mixture of cocoa, sugar and fat.

It took him years to find the best way to combine the ingredients.

His formula was later made by the Nestlé company. Milk chocolate is now popular all over the world.

Dark Chocolate

Dark chocolate is made without **milk solids**. It has a stronger taste than milk chocolate. Dark chocolate that has more cocoa in it is more **bitter**.

Dark chocolate has more health benefits than milk chocolate. It has more **nutrients** and less sugar and fat.

Dark chocolate can be **classified** as sweet dark, semi-sweet, or bittersweet.

White Chocolate

Although it is called chocolate, white chocolate isn't real chocolate at all. It doesn't contain cocoa powder like other forms of chocolate.

White chocolate is made from cocoa butter, **milk solids**, sugar, milk fat, and **lecithin**. It gets the light color from cocoa butter.

White chocolate is thought to have been first made in Switzerland in the 1930's as a way to use **excess** cocoa butter.

Nougat

Nougat is a sweet, sticky candy that is often found inside of chocolate bars.

White nougat is made with honey, sugar, and egg whites. Brown nougat is made mainly with honey and sugar. It does not contain eggs.

Many kinds of nougat are made with nuts. Adding different kinds of nuts or fruits changes the flavor.

Caramel

Caramel is a candy that is made up of melted sugar. To make caramel, sugar is melted slowly. As it melts, it **caramelizes**, which gives it the darker color and rich flavor.

Caramel is often added to chocolate bars and candies. It is also added to other desserts.

When making caramel, the caramel has to be stirred constantly. It is quick to burn if it is not stirred.

Nuts

Nuts are often added to chocolates. Pecans, almonds, and hazelnuts are some nuts that work well in chocolate.

Although they are often thought of as nuts, peanuts are actually **legumes**. They are very common in candy bars and chocolate treats.

Nuts add more protein to chocolate. They also increase the number of **calories**.

Truffles

Chocolate truffles are thought to have been first made in France. They were originally made up of a ball of chocolate **ganache** that is rolled in cocoa powder.

In America, any kind of chocolate candy that has a filling is often called a truffle.

Although chocolates that are filled with caramel, fruit cremes, or other fillings are often called truffles, they are not true truffles.

Baking

Chocolate is a very popular ingredient in many baked goods.

There are many different kinds of chocolate that can be used for baking. Chocolate chips are best used in cookies because they melt less than other chocolate.

Baking chocolate is unsweetened. It is meant to be used in recipes with added sugar. It can be used to make cakes, brownies, puddings, **ganache**, and more.

Chocolate Milk

Chocolate milk is thought to have been first made by Irish **botanist** Sir Hans Sloane in the early 1700's. He was in Jamaica and was given cocoa to drink.

He didn't like the taste, so he added some milk and made chocolate milk. It is now a very popular sweet drink.

Hot Chocolate

Hot chocolate is a rich, sweet drink. It is made from pieces or shavings of chocolate. It can be made with water, but it is creamier when made with milk.

Hot chocolate was first made by the Olmec, Aztec, and Mayan people of Central America.

Hot cocoa is **similar** to hot chocolate. It is made by mixing cocoa powder into hot water or milk.

Ice Cream

Ice cream is thought to have come from Naples, Italy in the 1600's. It is made with cream, milk, sugar, gelatin, and egg yolks.

Chocolate ice cream can be made by adding cocoa powder or melted chocolate to the mixture of other ingredients.

Ice cream can be made in many different flavors. The most popular flavors of ice cream are chocolate and vanilla.

Fudge

Fudge is thought to have been first made in America in the 1880's. It quickly became very popular in the area around New York and Massachusetts.

Fudge is very thick, rich, and smooth. It can be made in different flavors with things like nuts or fruit mixed in.

Fudge is full of lots of tiny sugar crystals. They are so small that fudge does not feel grainy.

Nutrition

Chocolate is high in fat and sugar. Dark chocolate is lower in **calories** than milk chocolate. It is often said to be a healthier treat than milk chocolate.

Chocolate does contain small amounts of **nutrients** such as vitamin E, calcium, phosphorus, and **antioxidants**.

Like other sugary treats, chocolate should be eaten in **moderation**.

Health Benefits

Dark chocolate is much healthier than milk chocolate or white chocolate. It is higher in **nutrients** and lower in fat and sugar.

The **flavanols** in dark chocolate can help to keep your skin **hydrated**, increase blood flow to the brain, and reduce the rick of heart disease.

In some studies, dark chocolate has been shown to lower blood pressure. This can help to keep your heart healthy.

Chocolate Festivals

Chocolate is a popular treat around the world. Many places have special festivals to celebrate chocolate.

At chocolate festivals, people can try different kinds of chocolate. There are cooking classes that teach people how to cook with chocolate.

People can buy chocolates at chocolate festivals. There are also displays of chocolate made by **chocolatiers.**

Recipes

Chocolate Fudge

Ingredients:

12 oz. semisweet chocolate chips

14 oz. sweetened condensed milk

1 cup chopped walnuts (optional)

Directions:

1. Combine chocolate chips and sweetened condensed milk in a medium saucepan. Heat on low, stirring until melted and smooth.

2. Remove from heat. Optional: add nuts.

3. Line 8x8 or 9x9 baking pan with foil.

4. Spread evenly in baking pan. Refrigerate about two hours or until firm.

5. Lift from pan and remove foil. Cut into small squares.

Chocolate Truffles

Ingredients:

8 ounces 60% chocolate

1/2 cup heavy cream

Sprinkles, melted chocolate, chopped nuts

Directions:

1. Finely chop chocolate.

2. Heat cream in a small saucepan until steaming. Pour over chocolate and allow to sit until melted.

3. Whisk mixture until it is smooth. Pour into a shallow baking pan and refrigerate about 30 minutes or until firm.

4. Use a tablespoon to scoop out chocolate. Roll into a ball and refrigerate until ready to top.

5. Roll the truffles in sprinkles, melted chocolate, or chopped nuts to top.

Glossary

Antioxidant: a substance that can help to repair cell damage

Bitter: having a sharp taste, not sweet

Botanist: someone who studies plants

Calories: units that measure the amount of energy a food can produce

Caramelize: to be made into caramel

Cocoa Liquor: a liquid form of chocolate made by grinding cocoa nibs

Chocolatier: a person or company who creates candies with chocolate

Classified: to group or order in classes

Excess: extra

Flavanols: substances found in some plants

Ganache: a whipped filling of chocolate and cream

Hydrated: to have enough water

Lecithin: a fat found in many foods that is important for our cells

Milk Solids: parts of milk that are separated from the liquid, including protein, lactose, and minerals

Moderation: not having too much

Nutrient: something in food that helps people to live and grow

Ointment: a cream that is rubbed into the skin

Similar: the same in some way, but not alike

About the Author

Victoria Blakemore is a first grade teacher in Southwest Florida with a passion for reading.

You can visit her at

www.elementaryexplorers.com

Also in This Series

Also in This Series